SL

MW01504196

Talking to Strangers

WHAT WE SHOULD KNOW ABOUT THE PEOPLE WE DON'T KNOW

By

MALCOLM GLADWELL

**Proudly Brought to you by
OneHour Reads**

Table of Contents

EXECUTIVE SUMMARY

There are books and there are books! *Talking to Strangers* is nothing short of powerful, insightful and highly revelatory. Behind many happenings and events lay theories to support claims and opinions put forward by people.

This book however demystifies many of these theories, especially with regards to how to talk to strangers. It tears the very fabric of what you should look out for when talking to strangers and replaces them with proven, real time instances that shape and redefine your outlook of the subject matter.

Talking to Strangers is not just a book. It is a tool for building successful and honest interpersonal relationships with those you know, as much as those you do not.

CHAPTER 1: FIDEL CASTRO'S REVENGE

KEY TAKEAWAYS

- Aspillaga was a man of repute
- Aspillaga had received a handwritten letter of commendation
- He had so much sensitive information about Cuba and the Soviet Union

The year was 1987, exactly two years before the fall of the Iron curtain. Florentino Aspillaga had his final posting in Bratislava, formerly known as Czechoslovakia. He ran a consulting company called Cuba Tecnica. The company was supposed to deal with trade and the likes, but honestly, it had nothing at all to do with trade. As a matter of fact, it was just a front. Aspillaga was a man of repute- a high-ranking officer in Cuba's General Directorate of Intelligence.

In 1985, Aspillaga had been named the intelligence officer of the year in the Cuban spy service. From Fidel Castro, Aspillaga had received a letter of commendation- handwritten. He was a National hero, one who had served his country brilliantly in different parts of the world. And here in Bratislava, he was responsible for overseeing Cuba's network of agents within the region.

However, at some point in his service, he became dissatisfied. He continually watched the Cuban leader; Castro deliver speeches in Angola as well as celebrate the revolution of the communist movement there. He was irritated by Castro's arrogance and narcissism, and by the time he was posted to Bratislava in 1986, his doubts had toughened.

Aspillaga planned to defect on June 6, 1987. This was hilarious, for June 6 was the anniversary of the founding of the Cuban Ministry of the Interior—the all-powerful body that administered the country's spy services. Hence, any worker within the General Directorate of Intelligence would naturally be celebrating on June 6. The day had a lot to mark it-speeches, receptions, ceremonies and all the usual stuff that come with celebrations. But Aspillaga had a different motive- he wanted his betrayal to sting.

Aspillaga had a girlfriend named Marta. One Saturday afternoon, he met with her in a park in downtown Bratislava. She was also Cuban, and worked in a Czech factory. Like many others of her kind, her passport was being held at the Cuban government offices in Prague. Owing to this, Aspillaga had no choice but to smuggle her across the border. Luckily for him, he ha a Mazda issued by the government. Intelligently, he took the spare tire out of the booth, cut a hole in the floor of the vehicle for air to pass through and told her to climb inside.

At this point in time, Eastern Europe was very much apart from the rest of the European continent. Travelling between the Eastern and Western points were under heavy restriction. However, the journey between Bratislava and Vienna was pretty short. Aspillaga had made that trip before. He was pretty known at the border, carrying his diplomatic passport. As he drove through, the guards waved at him.

On reaching Vienna, he, along with his girlfriend, Marta, abandoned the Mazda and hailed a taxi; presenting themselves at the United States Embassy. It was evening already, and all the senior staff were present at home. Getting the guard's attention was no uphill task, as Aspillaga only had to introduce himself as a case officer from Cuban Intelligence- a intelligence comandante.

Within the spy business, Aspillaga's action is known as a walk-in which is simply when an intelligence service official from a country unexpectedly shows up at the doorstep of the intelligence service of anther country. And be it as it may, Aspillaga was one of the renowned walk-ins of the Cold War. He had so much information; sensitive information about Cuba and the Soviet Union that following his defection from his former employers, he had been tracked down to be assassinated, twice. On both occasions, he escaped. Ever since, he had been spotted just once, by Brian Latell- the man who ran the Latin American office of the CIA for donkey years.

Latell got wind of Aspillaga's whereabout through an undercover agent who was acting as Aspillaga's intermediary. Latell met the intermediary at an eatery outside Miami, where he received instructions to meet in a different location which was closer to where Aspillaga was staying, under his new identity. In a hotel somewhere unknown, Latell rented a suite and waited for Aspillaga to arrive.

According to Latell, Aspillaga was much younger than him, even though he had terrible health challenges as a result of defecting and living with new identities from time to time. he however added that even though he looked diminished, Aspillaga must have ben a charismatic, slender, theatrical young man with a taste for risks and huge emotional gestures. When Aspillaga arrived the hotel suite, he was carrying a box which he set on the table and turned to Latell saying that the content of the box was a memoir he wrote shortly after he defected, and said he wanted Latell to have it.

In that box and the pages of the memoir lay a story with no sense in it.

Upon appearing at the American Embassy in Vienna, Aspillaga was flown to a debriefing center at a U.S. Army base in Germany. Now, at that time, American Intelligence functioned under the Swiss Flag, operating in Havana. Before Aspillaga began his debriefing, he made a request to the CIA to fly in a former Havana Station Chief whom the Cuban intelligence referred to as the Mountain Climber.

All over the world, the Mountain climber had dutifully served the CIA. When the Berlin Wall fell, files that were retrieved afterwards revealed that both the KGB and the East German secret police had taught a course on the Mountain climber to their agents. He was just too good. At some point in time, Soviet intelligence officers tried to recruit him by literally placing bags of money right in front of him. He was simply incorruptible as he waved them off and mocked them. Aspillaga had a role model, and it was the Mountain Climber. He wanted to meet with him, face-to-face.

The Mountain climber mentioned that he was on assignment in a different country when he received a message telling him to rush to Frankfurt. He recalled how a fellow had walked into the embassy and insisted on speaking with him. Straight, the Mountain Climber went to the debriefing center where he found four case officers sitted in the living room. He recalled being told that Aspillaga was in the bedroom making love with his girlfriend as he constantly had ever since his arrival. He remarked that despite Aspillaga's poor sense of dressing, one could easily tell that he was a very smart guy.

When Aspillaga came in, the mountain climber didn't reveal his identity; trying to be reticent. However, it did not take long before Aspillaga figured out who he was. The moment was golden, as they both hugged and shook hands the Cuban way.

They spoke for about five minutes before getting right to it. Shortly after, Aspillaga revealed the news that had brought him to the Vienna embassy. According to him, the CIA did have a strong network of spies within Cuba who had dutifully brought reports that helped shape America's understanding of its enemy. Naming one of them, Aspillaga reported that the agent was a double who worked for them, alongside. The entire room went silent. And then Aspillaga went on and on, reeling out names and descriptions of various agents, who practically made up the entire U.S. roster of secret agents inside Cuba. Each one of those men worked for Havana, while feeding the CIA information made up by the Cubans, themselves.

The mountain climber sat there, taking notes, while trying not to betray any emotion as they had been taught. But within himself, his heart was in a million places. All the people Aspillaga was mentioning were the Mountain Climber's people/ he had worked with all of these spies when he was posted to Cuba- a young, ambitious, intelligence officer. Upon his arrival in Havana, he made a point of overworking his sources, drilling them to provide information. He had always felt that if one had an agent in the office of the president of any country, and communication with such agent is inexistent, then the agent was worthless. So, in a bid to communicate and get value, he had dealt them a rather tough blow.

CHAPTER 2: GETTING TO KNOW der FÜHRER

KEY TAKEAWAYS

- Very few world leaders really knew who Hitler was.
- Chamberlain believed Hitler.
- The people who ended up being right about Hitler were those who had never met him personally.

The evening of August 28, 1938 had Neville Chamberlain call for his closest advisor. He was summoned for a late-night strategy meeting at 10 Downing Street. For a little more than a year, Chamberlain had been the British Prime Minister. He was a practical man, very plain spoken and he had interest in domestic affairs. He was also a former businessman. But all of these were nothing compared to what he had to face right now- a foreign-policy crisis, which was the first he'd be facing anyway. The crisis involved Adolf Hitler. At the time, Hitler had been making lots of warlike statements that tilted towards invading the German-speaking part of Czechoslovakia- Sudetenland.

If Germany made good its threat and invaded Czechoslovakia, it would result in nearly a world war, something which Chamberlain was trying to avoid at all possible costs. However, Hitler had remained withdrawn in recent months that Germany's motives were so unknown to the rest of Europe, causing them to grow anxious. Unhappy with the state of things, Chamberlain sought to resolve the stalemate. He had his idea, which was described as Plan Z dubbed and relayed to his advisors that night. This idea was top secret, and rather different from the norm. So different and unconventional was the idea that it took the foreign secretary, Halifax's breath away. Chamberlain wanted to go to Germany and meet with Hitler, face-to-face.

Now, there were a few weird things about the 1930s, one of which was the fact that very few people; very few world leaders really knew who Hitler was. He was a mystery. American president, Franklin Roosevelt never met Hitler. Neither did Soviet leader, Joseph Stalin. Winston Churchill came quite close in 1932 when he and Hitler made plans to meet. And both times, Hitler stood him up.

If there was any set of people that spent any real time with Hitler before the war commenced, it was the British aristocrats that were friendly to the Nazi's and who would occasionally cross over to join Hitler at parties. But even all of these were social calls. What Chamberlain was trying to do was to avert the world war, seeming to him that he would benefit from taking the measure of Hitler for himself. He really wanted to find out if Hitler was someone that could be trusted, and reasoned with.

September 14 came, and that morning, the British ambassador to Germany had a telegram sent to Hitler's foreign minister, Joachim von Ribbentrop, asking if Hitler would like to meet. The same day, a response came in positive. Chamberlain let the news out, disclosing that he would be going to Germany to meet with Hitler, and to see if he could avert the war. All around Britain, this sounded like a good thing with everyone, including the newspapers backing Chamberlain and making toasts to his health.

On the morning of September 15, Chamberlain left London. He had never flown before, but managed to remain calm all through the flight. At the airport, many had gathered to receive him. In a convoy of fourteen Mercedes, he was driven to the train station. Later on, he had lunch in Hitler's dining car while the train gradually made its way to Hitler's retreat at Berchtesgaden. He arrived at five in the evening. Hitler came and they share a handshake. According to Chamberlain, Hitler had brown hair and blue eyes with an altogether undistinguishable look; and one would never notice him in a crowd, but instead would mistake him for a house painter.

In the house, Chamberlain was ushered by Hitler into his study upstairs, followed by just an interpreter. At some point, Hitler exclaimed that he was ready to face a world war, making it plain that he was going to seize the Sudetenland, irrespective of what everyone else thought about his action. All Chamberlain wanted to know was if that was all that Hitler had planned, to which Hitler said it was. Chamberlain believed Hitler. He however failed to warn Hitler that if he went back on his promises, there would be consequences.

However, beneath all of those criticisms lay a puzzle. Chamberlain went two Germany on two more occasions, sitting and talking with Hitler for hours. In that period, Chamberlain was the only allied leader who actually got to spend significant time with Hitler. He made very detailed careful notes about Hitler's behavior, and ended up telling his cabinet back in

London that Hitler was a rational and determined man, as opposed to the crazy man they all thought him to be.

In all of these, Chamberlain as working on the assumption that we all follow in our efforts to make sense of strangers, believing that whatever information was garnered during personal interaction was somehow unique, and pretty valuable. Logically, no one would hire an employee without first getting to meet with them. Instead, they all do what Chamberlain did, look them in the eye, observe their demeanor, study their behavior intricately, and then, draw conclusions. Unfortunately, all that Chamberlain gathered from his interactions with Hitler didn't help him see Hitler better. Instead, it did the opposite.

One could conclude that this was because Chamberlain was naïve. Or perhaps because he had very little experience in foreign affairs.

This pattern, however, wasn't limited to Chamberlain. Lord Halifax also suffered the same fate. Halifax was everything that Chamberlain failed to be. He was a worldly, deeply seasoned, highly charming, intellectual man. He was also very religious.

In 1937, during fall, Halifax went to Germany where he met with Hitler. Besides Chamberlain, Halifax was the only other member of the ruling circle in Britain who got to spend time with Hitler. The meeting between the duo wasn't even premised on diplomatic relations. Instead, Halifax had mistaken Hitler for a footman, and almost given him his coat to hold. And for the next five hours, Hitler was himself, reeling out all about his hatred for the press, and the veils of the communist movement. Halifax listened to all of that.

Halifax spent a total of five days in Germany, where he met two of Hitler's top ministers- Hermann Göring and Joseph Goebbels. He also got to attend a dinner at the British Embassy, an avenue where he met lots of senior German businessmen and politicians. Upon returning home, Halifax said that everything was all to the good making contact with the German leadership, a statement that is difficult to disagree with. He did all that a diplomat ought to do: gain valuable insight from their face-to-face encounter. And like Chamberlain, he concluded that Hitler did not want ti go to war, and was very open to negotiating peace.

The third man on this rail is Nevile Henderson. Henderson spent the most time with Hitler as an ambassador to Germany. Hitler even had a nickname for him. In September 1938, like the two men before him, Henderson wrote that he had no thoughts whatsoever that suggest that Hitler had dishonorable intentions towards Czechoslovakia, and that he also believed that Hitler hated wars just as much as anyone else would. Sadly, like the other two, he read Hitler all wrong.

But this gets interesting. Hitler's case with these men had nothing to do with Hitler's ability to deceive some while revealing his true intentions to another. No. This is a situation about some people ending up being deceived by Hitler, while others simply didn't catch the bug. They just were able to see right through him, right past him and onto the truth. The only puzzle here is that those that were expected to be deceived were the ones who saw the truth, while those that one would expect to see the truth ended up being deceived.

For instance, Winston Churchill never for once believed that Hitler was any more than a deceitful rogue. He called Chamberlain's visit the most stupid thing anyone had ever done. Yet, all he did was read about Hitler. Duff Cooper was also on this page, listening to Chamberlain's meeting with Hitler in horror. He eventually resigned from Chamberlain's government in protest. And like Churchill, he also never met Hitler. Only Anthony Eden both met Hitler, and yet, saw past him to the truth. But this was not the case for everyone else. The people who ended up being right about Hitler were those who had never met him personally, while those who met him personally and talked with him for hours were usually wrong about him.

CHAPTER 3: THE QUEEN OF CUBA

KEY TAKEAWAYS

- Lots of Cubans fled the Fidel Castro regime.
- Hermanos al Rescate rescued several lives.
- The Cuban Air force shot down two Hermanos al Rescate airplane, killing four people.

In the early 1990's, lots of Cubans began to flee the Fidel Castro regime. They made boats, as crude as they were, and set out on voyages to the United States. On the average, not less than twenty-four thousand people died while making the journey. It was a total human-rights disaster. Responding to the happening, a group of Cuban emigrés in Miami founded what was known as Hermanos al Rescate, which means Brothers to the Rescue. They put together an air force team and began searching for refugees from the air, and radioing their coordinates to the Coast Guard. They rescued tons of lives. They became heroes.

As time went by, the emigrés became more ambitious. They started to fly into Cuban airspaces, and they began dropping leaflets on Havana stirring the Cubans to rise up against Castro's regime. Already mortified by the flight of refugees, the Cuban government was livid. Tensions rose on all sides, and finally came to an end on February 24, 1996. One that fateful afternoon, three planes belonging to Hermanos al Rescate took off, heading for the Florida Straits. As they approached the Cuban coastline, both planes were shot at by two Cuban Air Force MIG fighter jets, killing all four people aboard the planes instantly.

Response to this action came immediately. The United Nations Security Council had passed a resolution that denounced the Cuban government. President Clinton held a press conference. In Miami, the Cuban emigré population was mad. Both planes had been shot in international airspace, an act that could be said to be one of war. However, in the midst of the ongoing controversy, the story changed. Eugene Carroll, a retired U.S real admiral granted an interview to CNN. He was a key figure within Washington, and had previously served as the director of all U.S. armed forces in with nothing less than seven thousand weapons at his disposal. Before the shoot down, he revealed that himself and a small group of military analysts had met with top Cuban officials. He disclosed that they were hosted by the Ministry of Defense. He also added that the traveled around and inspected Cuban bases and schools, the power plant that was yet to be completed and a host of others. Interestingly, he mentioned that questions came up about the overflights from the U.s Aircrafts- private, not government aircrafts operating out of Miami. He was asked what would happen if one of those were shot down. Carroll stated that he interpreted that question from his hosts as a warning in disguise. And upon returning back to his base, he discussed the information with the member of the State Department and members of the Defense Intelligence Agency.

The Defense Intelligence Agency, otherwise known as the DIA, is an arm of the foreign intelligence threesome in the United States government- the third of the trio precisely, in addition to the CIA and the National Security Agency. Now, if Carroll had actually met with the DIA and the State department, then he had delivered the warning to the highest security bodies in the American government. But did the state department ad DIA take those warnings seriously, and attempt to stop the Hermanos al Rescate from being reckless? No, they did not.

All around Washington DC, Carroll's comments reverberated. It was embarrassing. The shoot down happened on the 24th of February, and Carroll's warning had been relayed on the 23rd of February.

In all of these, Fidel Castro was not invited onto CNN to defend his case. There was no need for him to do that anyway. A rear admiral was already making his case.

The next three chapters of this book are dedicated to the ideas of a psychologist who goes by the name Tim Levine. Levine had thought widely about the problem of why we are deceived by strangers as much as anyone in the social sciences as. In the second chapter, we get to look through his theories, particularly through the Bernie Madoff story. Madoff is the investor who successfully ran the largest Ponzi scheme ever recorded in history. The third chapter examines the rather unusual case of Jerry Sandusky- a football coach in Pennsylvania, who was convicted of sexual abuse. The first is this- the end result of the crisis between Cuba and the United states in 1996.

You may wonder if there are oddly- striking events bout Admiral Carroll and the Cuban shoot downs, and you would not be far from being right. There are too many coincidences here. first off, the Cubans plan to launch an attack on citizens of the United states flying in international airspace. Next up, it magically happens that the day before the attack takes place, an influential military man who is an insider sternly warns the U.S officials about the possibility of such an action being executed. Incidentally, that warning puts the very same official in a place to make the Cuban cases on one of the world's most respected news networks, the following day.

All of these timings are too perfect, to some extent, you would agree with me. I mean, if you look at this from a public relations angle, a public relations firm trying to mute the fallout from a very controversial action would most likely script the events like this. And this is exactly what Reg Brown, a military counterintelligence analyst thought to himself, in the days that followed after the incident. Now, Brown worked with the Defense Intelligence Agency on the Latin desk. And his job was majorly understanding the ways the Cuban intelligence services tried to influence American military operations. Simply put, what he had to do was to be attentive and alert to the very little details that many of us would ignore. The intricacies, tinges and the coincidences that everyone else would ignore. And somehow, Brown couldn't let go of the thought that the Cubans might have planned the entire crisis.

As fate would have it, it was eventually revealed that the Cubans did have an insider within the Hermanos al Rescate. He was a pilot named Juan Pablo Roque. The day preceding the attack, he had mysteriously disappeared and resurfaced at Castro's end in Havana. He mentioned to his bosses back in Havana that the Hermanos al Rescate had something planned for the 24th. This twist made it difficult for Brown to believe that the date of the Carroll briefing was chosen by chance. On a normal day, in order to have the best public relations effect, the Cubans would want their warning out a day before the attack. This way, it would be impossible for the DIA and the state department to say that the warning wasn't clear enough, or the time difference was too far apart. Carroll's words were right in their faces on the day the pilots took off from Miami.

The next step was to find out the person that arranged the meeting. Brown did some investigation and was shocked to find out that it was a colleague of his at the DIA, Ana Belen Montes. Now, Ana Montes wasn't just anybody within the DIA. She was a superstar. She had received several awards and accolades over the years. She was even described by her former boss from the Department of Justice, as the best employee he ever had. And within the intelligence community, she was nicknamed the Queen of Cuba. So, how and why could she?

Brown was distraught. He couldn't just go out there levelling an accusation against his colleague without concrete fact. He finally decided to meet with a DIA counterintelligence officer named Scott Carmichael, to whom he bared his thoughts. Like him, Carmichael also did not want to do anything wrong.

Carmichael drew him out slowly. Over time, the Cubans had proved to be really good at their craft. And Brown did have his own evidence. Sometime in the late 1980's, Brown had written a report on a number of Cuban officials who were directly involved in drug smuggling, providing all the specifics there could ever be. And just a few days before the report was released, the Cubans rounded up each and every individual mentioned in his report, executed some of them and denied it publicly. There was a leak.

Brown had lots of reasons to be suspicious. He went on to tell Carmichael the other event that took place during the Hermanos al Rescate crisis. Ana Montes worked at the DIA's office in Washington DC. When the planes went under, she was called into the Pentagon. Now, this shooting occurred on a Saturday. The evening after, Brown called asking for Montes, and he was told that she had left. According to the woman who picked the phone, Montes got a call earlier that day, and she became nervous. Afterwards, she told everyone in the situation room that she was tired, and since nothing was going on at the time, she left for home. To Brown, this was absolutely ridiculous. Nobody leaves the pentagon under a crisis situation, and definitely not because you are hungry and tired. It just did not check.

Months passed. Carmichael requested to speak with Montes. All her stories checked. The meeting was not her idea. She arranged the meeting on the 23rd of February 'cos it was convenient for them both. She could not remember piking a call in the situation room, but she had allergies, and on a Sunday the cafeteria in the Pentagon would not open. She had gone all day without eating. All her lines seemed to check.

Five years later however, it was discovered that every night Ana Montes went home, she had typed up from her memory all of the facts and insights she had learned that day from work, sending them to her handlers in Havana.

From her very first day as an employee of the DIA, she had been a Cuban spy.

CHAPTER 4: THE HOLY FOOL

KEY TAKEAWAYS

- Madoff was an unusually secretive man.
- Madoff was the brain behind the biggest Ponzi scheme ever.
- When you default to truth, you create a problem.

In 2003, November to be precise, Nat Simons sent a mail to a number of his colleagues at the Long Island-based hedge fund Renaissance Technologies. There was a pretty complicated stake of financial arrangements and the company was caught up staked in a fund operated by a New York investor. The investor was known as Bernard Madoff, and Madoff did make Simons uncomfortable.

Perhaps if you worked in the New York financial sphere between the late 1990s and early 2000s, you might have heard of Bernard Madoff. Madoff worked in the Lipstick building, and served as a board member on several reputable financial-industry association. He was sleek, moving amongst the affluent circles. But there was something that made Simons very uncomfortable about him. He was secretive. Simons had heard rumors from someone he trusted. And going by what he wrote in the mail, whoever this person was already said that Madoff would have serious problems within a year. He mentioned that if you threw in the fact that his brother-in-law is his auditor, and that his son was also a top gun in the organisation, then there were risks of some nasty allegations and freezing of accounts.

The following day, one of the firm's top executives, Henry Laufer responded, agreeing that Renaissance did have some independent evidence; suggesting that indeed, something was unusual about Madoff. The risk manger for the Renaissance company, Paul Broder also sent a detailed analysis of the trading strategy that Madoff claimed to adopt for his business, and it still did not add up. At this point, all three men decided they would conduct an investigation all by themselves, in-house. Renaissance already had doubts about Madoff and what his business was about, as they had no idea how he was making his money. According to Broder, the figures he was churning out were unsupported by any evidence that was found.

One would think that Renaissance would sell off its stake in Madoff, but instead, they cut their stake in half, and hedged their bets. Five years later, after it had been brought to the limelight that Madoff was a fraud and the brain behind the biggest Ponzi scheme ever, federal investigators had a sit-down with Nat Simons and asked him to provide explanations as to why. And according to Simons, he just never thought that Madoff was being fraudulent. He did admit that he had no understanding of what Madoff was actually up to, and that, yeah, Madoff did smell quite funny. But he had no reason to believe that Madoff was that much a liar. So yeah, Simon did have doubts, but since they were not strong enough, he dodged to truth.

In a routine audit by the Securities and Exchange Commission, SEC, e-mails exchanged between Simons and Laufer were discovered. This wasn't the first time that SEC had questioned Madoff's operations.

What Madoff claimed was that he followed an investment strategy linked to the stock market. This simply meant that like any other market-based strategy, his returns would go up and down, just like the market. But this was not the case with Madoff's returns. They were rock steady, defying all logical explanations. An investigator from SEC, by the name Peter Lamore once met with Madoff to get explanations as regards this. And all that Madoff said was that he could see beyond the surface and around corners, and that he had a super gut feel that he knew just when to get out of the market before a crash, and when to return into the market before a rise. Lamore mentioned that he asked him repeatedly, because he also felt that this gut feeling was rather suspicious. And Lamore did think that there was more, and that perhaps, Madoff had some insight in the overall board market that others did not have.

He then took his doubts to his boss, who shared the same doubts as well. His boss, Robert Sollazo also had questions that were unanswered about Madoff. However, these doubts were not enough. Even after SEC conducted its investigations and waved off Madoff's claim on the gut feel as necessarily ridiculous, Sollazo still did not think it was. But SEC already defaulted to truth, and the fraud continued. And it was not just on Wall Street, a lot of people who had one thing or the other to do with Madoff just felt that something was amiss. Even the real-estate broker who rented him an office space. However, no one did anything about how they felt, or what they thought, neither did anyone conclude that they were dealing with the world's greatest con man, ever. In his case, everyone succumbed to truth. Everyone, besides one person.

Sometime in 2009, early February, a man known as Harry Markopolos stated at a nationally televised hearing before congress. Markopolos was an independent fraud investigator, who spoke with a New York accent. Before then, no one even knew who he was. And so he began by talking about how himself and his team tried to get the SEC to examine, investigate and put an end to the Madoff Ponzi scheme, repeatedly sending the body warnings from May 2000. According to Markopolos, himself and a few of his colleagues had created charts and graphs, ran computer models and poked around in Europe, where Madoff raised the bulk of his money. They knew that they had provided enough red flags and mathematical proofs to the SEC to enable them shut Madoff down there and then when he was valued at under seven billion dollars. The SEC did nothing then, and Markopolos returned in 2001, 2005, 2007 and 2008, with each attempt leading him nowhere. He was frustrated.

Amongst the tons of people who had doubts about Madoff, Harry Markopolos was the only one who did not default to truth and saw the stranger for who he was. And just while his hearing was mid-way gone, one of the congressmen offered Markopolos an opportunity to come to Washington and run the SEC. Markopolos is one man that we all can learn from. When you default to truth, you create a problem. This way, spies and con artists go scot free.

CHAPTER 5: CASE STUDY: THE BOY IN THE SHOWER

KEY TAKEAWAYS

- Sandusky, the most hated man in America.
- Sandusky denies being sexually attracted to young, underage boys.

The date was March 21, 2017. It was a court session. Michael McQueary was being examined by the prosecution where he was asked if he saw something unusual occur while he was a graduate assistant in 2001. He went on to recount the occurrence to the jury.

According to McQueary, one night, he gently made his way to the Lasch Football building and proceeded to one of the locker rooms in the building. Upon opening the locker room door, he heard showers running as well as slapping sounds. He realized someone was in the locker room, taking a shower. But the slapping sounds caused him to realize that what was going on was more than just a shower. The time was 8:30pm, and it was a Friday night. Looking over his right shoulder, he sees a man standing naked over a minor individual, of between ten to twelve years of age. Both of them were naked. And then a name fell out of his mouth, as he identified the older individual as Jerry, right up against the young boy, stomach to back.

The Jerry that was being referred to was Jerry Sandusky. Sandusky had just retired as the defensive coordinator of the Penn State football team. He was a well-loved figure at Penn State, and McQueary had known him for quite some years. McQueary immediately ran to his office and placed a call across to his parents. He reported what he had seen. According to McQueary's father, his son was shaken by the incident. As a matter of fact, even his mom was able to detect that something was wrong with McQueary over the call.

Following what he saw in the shower that day, McQueary went to his boss, Joe Paterno and reported the incident to him. He explained in detail what he had seen, describing that he saw the coach have skin-on-skin contact with the young boy. He also mentioned that he heard slapping sounds coming from the shower room. And the reaction that McQueary received from Paterno was one of sadness, with Paterno slumping back into his chair and his face going dim.

Paterno went on to report the case to his own boss who happened to be the athletic director at Penn State, Tim Curley. Curley went on to mention the event to Gary Schultz, a senior administrator at the university. Together, both men took the case to the University's president, Graham Spanier, after which an investigation was launched. And in due course, Sandusky was apprehended and while he was facing trial, a superb, unbelievable story was brought forward. A total of eight young men testified to having been molested by Sandusky at various points in time in hotel rooms, locker room showers and even in his own home, while his wife was upstairs. He ended up being convicted of child molestation on forty-five counts, with over a hundred million dollars paid in settlement to his victims by Penn State. A book written on the case was titled the most hated man in America, which really was what Sandusky became.

This is not where it gets interesting however. The one thing that's intriguing in this whole episode is the phrase that says in due course. It was in the year 2001 that McQueary saw Sandusky in the shower. It took almost ten years before an investigation into Sandusky's character commenced. Nd his arrest didn't even come until November 2011. Why did it take forever? When Sandusky got jailed, the lights beamed on the leadership of the University. The school's football coach, Joe Paterno, resigned out of disgrace. Shortly afterwards, he died. And a statue of him erected a few years before then was taken down. The two senior administrators of the University, Gary Schultz and Tim Curley were both charged with conspiracy, obstruction of justice as well as failure on their part to report a child abuse case. They both went to jail as well. And lastly, the University's president was not left out of the scandal. He had been President for sixteen years, transforming the school's reputation, academically. Unfortunately, in November 2011, he was fired. And six years down the drain, he was imprisoned for child endangerment.

During the period when the controversy was heated, Sandusky granted an interview to Bob Costas, NBC sports anchor. Costas made a direct statement to Sandusky, saying that the former claimed he was no pedophile to which Sandusky remarked that Costas was right. Costas the went on to mention that Sandusky had admitted to showering with young boys, and sought to find out how all of his inappropriate behaviors among these young boys excluded him from being a pedophile. Sandusky, in his response to Costas mentioned that he had strong interest in the lives of young people, and therefore did all he could to connect with them. After defending himself against being a pedophile for a long time, Costas asks if Sandusky is sexually attracted to young, underage boys, which Sandusky denied.

The real deal here is: just like the Ana Montes, Bernie Madoff and Harry Markopolos cases that reveal just how difficult it is for us to overcome defaulting to the truth, would you as the President of Penn State, having been confronted with the same sets of facts and questions have behaved any differently from Spanier who continually allowed Sandusky roam freely around the University campus?

The very first question about Sandusky's conduct was birthed in 1998 when a Second Mile boy came home with his hair wet. According to the kid, he had worked out with Sandusky and afterwards, they had both taken a shower in the locker room. The boy added that Sndusky had wrapped his arms around him and said that he was gonna squeeze the little boy's guts out. In addition, Sandusky then lifted him to get the soap out of his air, while the little boy's feet touched Sandusky's thigh. The mother, uncomfortable about the happening mentioned it to her child's psychologist, Alycia Chambers. However, she was not sure what to make of the incident. She continually asked if she was overreacting. Meanwhile, her son saw nothing wrong, describing himself as the luckiest boy in the world because he got to sit on the Sidelines at Penn State football games when he was with Sandusky. That closed the case.

The next incident involved a boy named Aaron Fisher, who came from a troubled home. He had gotten really familiar with Sandusky, spending couple of nights at Sandusky's home. His mother always thought of Sandusky as an angel, until the boy mentioned in November 2008 that he felt uncomfortable with some of Sandusky's behavior.

CHAPTER 6: THE FRIENDS FALLACY

KEY TAKEAWAYS

- In FACS, each of the forty-three different muscle movements in the face gets assigned a number.
- Those trained in FACS can look at an individual's facial expressions and simply score them

By the time Friends was in its fifth season, it was inching closer to becoming one of the most successful shows ever recorded. It belonged to the class of the great hang out comedies, featuring six friends- Monica, Rachel, Phoebe, Joey, Chandler, and Ross who lived in a chaos ridden jumble somewhere in Downtown Manhattan, majorly talking hilariously.

At the beginning of the season, Ross gets married to an outsider; outside the Friends' network. By the time the season gets to the middle, the relationship ends, and by the end of the season, he gets back in Rachel's arms where he has now found love. Phoebe begets triplets and hooks up with a police officer. Monica and Chandler end up falling in love- creating a problem in the immediate because Monica is Ross's sister, and Chandler is Ross's best friend, and both of them had not the courage to tell Ross what is going on. When episode fifteen begins, Monica and Chandler can no longer hold their ploy together. Ross, while looking out the window sees his sister, Monica in a romantic embrace with his friend, Chandler. He's shocked to his marrows, as he runs to Monica's apartment and tries to barge in. However, the chain is on her door, and ha has no choice but to stick his face through the tiny gap between the door and the chain. In fury he shouts out to Chandler, alerting him that he saw what was going on through the window.

Chandler is scared and tries to escape through the window. Monica prevents him from doing so, saying she can handle her brother, Ross. She goes on to open the door, and attempts to start a meaningful conversation with Ross. Immediately Ross comes in, he launches at Chandler and begins chasing him around the kitchen. Chandler hides behind Monica, while Joey and Rachel run in. Rachel seeks to find out what is going on, and Chandler responds saying he thinks Ross knows about himself and Monica. Ross goes on in anger, saying he thought Chandler was his best friend, and he could not believe his nest friend was entangled in an affair with his sister.

Now this is what's important. Friends was just a regular show, but a standard season of the show recorded several twists and turns of plots. It also revealed varying narratives and emotions, seeming as though viewers of the show would require some help so they don't lose their way. In the real sense of things however, it was almost impossible that anyone would get confused. The show was as clear as day. I would like to say that the show was so clear that one could understand it without turning the sound up.

The second puzzle that this book examines is the bail problem. Somehow, judges who know much more about defendants do a poor job of evaluating them than a computer program will. This section is an attempt to answer the puzzle, and it begins with the weird fact of how crystal-clear television shows like Friends are.

In a bid to test the idea of transparency of Friends, I reached out to a psychologist known as Jennifer Fugate. Fugate is a lecturer with the University of Massachusetts at Dartmouth. Fugate is an expert in FACS, which stands for Facial Action Coding System (FACS).

In FACS, each of the forty-three different muscle movements in the face gets assigned a number. This number is referred to as an action unit. People who are trained in FACS, like Fugate, can look at an individual's facial expressions and simply score them; the same way a musician would listen to a piece of music and translate it into tons of notes on the page. FACS is extraordinary. With this system, details of muscular movements are catalogued. FACS has a manual which consists of over five hundred pages. If Fugate had attempted analyzing the entire episode, it would have taken days. as a result, I told her to focus only on the opening scene where Ros sees Chandler and Rachel embracing, and then rushes over in anger.

Fugate found out that the minute Ross looked through the crack in the door, and sees his sister embracing his friend in a romantic way, his face reveals action units of 10 + 16 + 25 + 26: That's the upper-lip raiser - levator labii superioris, caput infraorbitalis; the lower-lip depressor -depressor labii, parted lips- depressor labii, relaxed mentalis or orbicularis oris, and jaw drop- relaxed temporal and internal pterygoid. In addition to being given action units, muscular movements are also given intensity measure from A to E, A being the mildest of all while E, the strongest. In that moment, all of Ross's movements were Es. And if you are opportune to see that episode of Friends again, while freezing at the screen the moment when Ross looks through the door crack, then you'll see the exact thing the FACS coders are referring to. On his face stood a look of complete anger and disgust, one that could not be mistaken for anything else.

Transparency as a concept has a very long history. In the year 1872, thirteen years from the time Charles Darwin presented his famous discourse on evolution, the renowned scientist published the expressions of the emotions in man and animals. In his publication, he argued that smiling, frowning and wrinkling noses inn disgust were things every human being did as a part of evolutionary adaptation. He argued further that accurately and speedily communicating emotions from one human to the other was of so much importance to the survival of the human species, and hence, the face had seemingly developed into a billboard for the heart.

This idea of Darwin's is deeply profound. Let's take a look at this. When children are happy, they smile everywhere they go. When they are sad, they frown. When they are amused, they giggle. And so, it's not just those who watch Friends that can make sense of the feelings passed around by Rossa and Rachel. Everyone can. In chapter two, the bail hearings by the judge do not tally with the parties in a court case. But they are also an exercise in transparency. A major belief held by judges is that it is important to look at the people they are judging. In a lawsuit some years ago, a Muslim woman in Michigan was the plaintiff. She came to court wearing her niqab, which is a traditional outfit for Muslim women. The judge asked that she took it off, but she refused to. And the judge simply dismissed her case. He told her point blank that he did not think he could fairly judge a disagreement between two different parties when he could see one of them, but not the other. Without mincing words, he told her that there were certain things about her demeanor and temperament that he has to see in a court of law.

CHAPTER 7: A SHORT EXPLANATION OF THE AMANDA KNOX CASE

KEY TAKEAWAYS

- Guede had a criminal history.
- The Amanda Knox case was completely different from other signature crime cases.
- The Amanda Knox case is one of transparency.

November 1, 2017 was the murder of Meredith Kercher by Rudy Guede. It was at night. It too some arguments, speculations and controversy to prove, but eventually, it became certain that he was guilty as alleged. Guede was a shady person who had been hanging around the house in Perugia, Italy. Kercher lived there. Kercher was student in college, and she lived in the house during a year abroad. Guede didn't have a clean slate. He did have a criminal history. He admitted to being in Kercher's house the night she was murdered, but had the most unlikely reasons as to why. The entirety of the crime scene had his DNA on it. And after Kercher's body was discovered, Guede fled Italy for Germany.

However, Guede was not the sole focus of the police investigation, neither was he seriously in their thoughts following the discovery of Kercher's body. Instead, the focus was on Amanda Knox who happened to be Kercher's roommate. Amanda had come home one morning and found blood in the bathroom. Together with her boyfriend, Rafelle Sollecito, they called the police. When the police came, they found Kercher lying dead in her bedroom, and it only became a matter of hours before Amanda and Sollecito were added to their list of suspects. The police believed that the crime was a drug- and alcohol-fueled sex game which went south, and that Guede, Knox and Sollecito were involved. All three of them were arrested, charged, convicted and from there on, sent to prison. The press kept tabs on each step of the procedure.

Funny thing is, many other signature crime stories are enthralling when you get to rediscover them years later. However, this case is a complete exception. For starters, there was no physical evidence that tied Knox or her boyfriend to the crime. There was also no logical explanation as to why Knox, a young immature, middle-class girl from Seattle would be interested in engaging in such dangerous games with someone she barely even knew. The police investigation which was revealed against her was highly shocking. The DNA which was analyzed, and which supposedly linked Knox and her boyfriend to the crime was completely inferior. Her prosecutor was no better, as he dwelt on his obsession and fantasies about elaborate sex crimes. And it took eight solid years after the crime for Knox to be declared innocent. And even at that, many people one would have considered intelligent and thoughtful disagreed with the judgement; and on the day she was released from prison, an angry mob gathered in the town square, protesting against her release. Logically, this case makes no sense.

I could go ahead and offer you a detailed analysis of what was wrong with the investigation that was done concerning Kercher's murder. In fact, I could easily refer you to some really comprehensive analysis done by scholars, on this subject matter. I would spare you all of those and give you the simplest and shortest theory of the Amanda Knox case. The Amanda Knox case is one of transparency. Now if you do believe that the way a stranger looks and acts is a vital and dependable clue as to the way they feel; if you believe the Friends fallacy- then, you're bound to make mistakes. One of such mistakes was Amanda Knox.

There is this kind of experiment that social scientists often do, where you have a sender who is the subject and a judge. Now, what you want to do is to measure how accurate the judge is at spotting the sender's lies. Levine, whom we read about in the second chapter discovered the same thing that psychologists often discover in cases like these- many of us are not so good at detecting lies. An average estimation puts judge's ability to correctly identify liars at 54 per cent, just slightly above chance. And this remains the case, regardless of who is judging. Everyone is terrible- students, the FBI, CIA officers, lawyers. Truth be told, there may be some people who are exceptionally good at detecting lies and liars. But if they do exist, they are definitely rare and this is why.

The first is that for very good reasons, we end up giving people the benefit of the doubt and assume that those we are talking to are honest individuals. However, Levine was unsatisfied with that explanation. The problem is much deeper and larger than simply defaulting to truth. As a matter of fact, Levine found out that lies are usually detected much later, in some cases, weeks, and others months or even years later.

For instance, when Scott Carmichael told Ana Montes during their first meeting that he had no reason to suspect that she might have been involved in a counterintelligence influence operation, she sat there simply looking at him. She just stat there. However, in hindsight, Carmichael felt that if she was innocent, she would have done something- maybe cried or protested, but she simply did nothing, except sit there. In that instant, however, Carmichael missed that clue. It was only by chance that Montes was caught, four years after. What Levine found is that in the moment, we often miss the very vital clues. And this singular discovery puzzled him. Why? What is it that happens at that instant that a lie is told that derails us in particular? And in a bid to find an answer to this, Levine returned to his tapes.

In one of the videos Levine showed me, there was a young woman whom I'd address as Sally. Levine walked her through the straightforward questions without incident. And then, the crucial moment came, and Levine went straight to ask if any cheating occurred when Rachel left the room. She responded with a categorical No. he asked if she was telling the truth, and she said Yes. Then, Levine mentioned that if he interviewed her partner, he was going to ask the same question. He then turned to Sally and asked what her partner was going to say to which Sally responded that her partner was probably going to give the same answer as she did. You see, the moment Levine asked Sally if any cheating occurred, Sally's arms and face began to take on a bright red color. It would do no justice to call it a bright red. What Sally actually did was to give a whole new meaning to the expression of being caught red-handed. Then the critical question comes, and Sally is asked what her partner would say. Even whilst blushing, Sally still could not come up with a convincing line that says her partner would agree with her. Instead, she weakly says her partner would probably agree with her. Fact is, at the point where she begins to blush, Sally is lying, and all called in to judge the tape realized she is lying.

CHAPTER 8: CASE STUDY: THE FRATERNITY PARTY

KEY TAKEAWAYS

- One in every five American female college students say that they have been the victim of sexual assault.
- The transparency assumption is also a problem for teenagers and young adults
- On every issue, there are divergent opinions amongst males and females.

It was January 18, 2015 in Palo Alto, California. The time was just around midnight. Two Swedish graduates are cycling across Stanford University Campus, headed for a fraternity party. Just about ten, they notice what appears to be two people lying outside a fraternity house while a party is fully going on. So as not to disturb the couple, they slowed down, thinking it was a personal moment for them both. As they drew closer, they realized that the man was atop a young woman.

The prosecution lawyer asked Peter Johnson, one of the students, what he saw. Peter responded saying they saw a man on top of a woman, or at most, a man on top of another person very close to the Kappa Alpha house. When asked if he saw any movement or motion from the person on top, Peter replied that initially, the man was only moving a little bit, but later on, he started thrusting with greater intensity. As for the person at the bottom, he said whoever it was did nothing, but just laid there. Johnson and Carl-Fredrik Arndt got off their bikes and moved closer. Johnson called out to the man who lifted his body and looked up at them. Johnson continued to move closer, causing the man to get up. He began to back away. Almost immediately, Johnson asked him what he was doing, especially because he realized that the girl was unconscious, he asked one more time what the man was doing, and afterwards, the man began to run. Johnson and his friend ran after him and tackled him. The man that was tackled was Brock Turner, a nineteen-year-old freshman at Stanford. He was also a member of the University's swim team. Less than an hour before, he had met a young woman at the Kappa Alpha party. Later on, Turner would disclose to the police that they had both danced together, gone outside and lad down on the ground. The woman, on the other hand was a recent graduate from college, and her name was Emily Doe. She had come to the party with a bunch of friends. At this point in time however, she lay unconscious underneath a pine tree. Her skirt had been pushed up to her waist, and her underwear was on the floor, right next to her. The top of her dress had been pulled down partially, exposing one of her breasts. A few hours later, when she came around in the hospital, a police officer told her that she might have been sexually assaulted. She was confused, and got up. She went to the bathroom and discovered that her underwear was gone. It had been taken for evidence.

After she used the bathroom, she felt some scratching on her neck, she realized that it was pine noodles. She even thought she may have fallen from a tree, and had no idea why she was in the hospital. The prosecution lawyer then asked if there was a mirror in the bathroom. She said there was. He went on to ask if she could see her hair in the mirror. She said Yes. The prosecution lawyer then asked her to describe how her hair appeared. In response, she said her hair was just unkempt and had little stuff poking out of it. Asked if she had any idea how her hair ended up like that, she said she did not. Finally, the prosecution lawyer asked her what she did after he used the restroom, and she said she went back to the bed. According to her, she was given a blanket, she wrapped herself, and went back to sleep.

In the world at large, on a yearly basis, there are lots of encounters just like this one that ended so terribly on the lawn outside the Kappa Alpha Fraternity on Stanford University. On several occasions, two young people who are otherwise strangers to one another meet and engage in conversations. Such conversations could be brief, or they could go on for hours unending. These two people might end up going home together, or things might be close to that, but end. At some point in the evening, things may go really south. An estimated one in five American female college students say that they have been the victim of sexual assault. A good percentage of those cases follow this pattern. In these kinds of cases, the challenge is largely reconstructing the pattern. There are several questions to ponder upon. Did both parties consent to it, only one party did? Was there some misunderstanding? Truth is, if the transparency assumption remains a problem for police officers making sense of suspects, or judges who try to read defendants, then, it definitely would be a problem for teenagers and young adults trying to find their way through a complex web of human domains.

A survey was carried out in 2015 by the Washington Post/Kaiser Family foundation. A thousand university students were surveyed, and asked whether they thought certain behaviors established consent for more sexual activity. The behaviors ranged from taking off their own clothes to getting a condom and the likes. This is the real deal. If all college students agreed that by getting a condom, one implicitly consents to sex, then consent would be a straightforward matter. If the rules are clearly laid out, each party can easily understand and infer accurately what the other person wants and is comfortable with by reason of their behavior. But results from the poll reveals that there are no rules to this. On every issue, there are divergent opinions amongst males and females. In some cases, there are men who think like some women do, and vice versa. There are also men who think in one direction, and women who think in the opposite direction. And there are those, present among both genders, who hold no opinion at all.

What would it mean when half of the young men and women say they are unclear about whether a clear agreement is necessary for sexual activity? Does it mean that they haven't thought about it before? Does it mean that they would rather proceed on a case-by-case basis? Does it mean they reserve the right to sometimes proceed without explicit consent, and at other times to insist on it? The legal system was mystified by the Amanda Knox case because the way she acted and the way she felt just did not add up. But this is transparency failure on steroids. When a student in college meets another, even in situations where they have genuinely honest intentions, the burden of accurately interpreting sexual intentions is a gamble. And like Lori Shaw asks, how is it that we expect students to respect boundaries that have no universal agreement as to what they are?

A complicating element in all of these however is that when you read through all of the details of the campus sexual-assault cases, which by the way have become so rampant, there is a remarkable fact which usually involves a near, identical scenario. In many cases, it is the story of a young man and woman who meet a party, and who go on to disastrously misinterpret one another's intentions, both of them, drunk.

CHAPTER 9: KSM WHAT HAPPENS WHEN THE STRANGER IS A TERRORIST?

KEY TAKEAWAYS

- Mukhtar meant the brain
- Mukhtar was one of the most senior Al Qaeda guys ever captured
- Transparency on the other hand is a commonsense assumption which has turned out to be more of an illusion

James Mitchell's first response was that the man looked like a troll. He said he was glaring at him, angry and aggressive. James Mitchell said he was probing him neutrally, same way he would if he were talking to anyone else. James mentioned that the man took the hood off and he (Mitchell) asked him what he would like to be called.

The man answered him, saying he should call him Mukhtar. He said that Mukhtar meant the brain, and that he was the emir of the 9/11 attacks. And from then on, Mitchell began to recount.

It was March 2001, in a CIA black site someplace in the world. Mukhtar was KSM, and he was one of the most senior Al Qaeda guys ever captured. He was without clothes, completely naked. His hands and feet were in chains, yet he was defiant. At this point, all Mukhtar's head and beard had been completely shaved off. Mitchell mentioned that Mukhtar was the hairiest person he had ever seen. And that he had a very huge belly. He wondered if Mukhtar did kill all those Americans.

Mitchell himself had the build of a runner. He was tall and slender, and had his hair parted in the middle. His beard was also neatly trimmed. He did describe himself as looking like one guy's uncle.

By training, Mitchell is a psychologist. After the 9/11 attacks, Mitchell and his colleague, Bruce Jessen were brought in by the CIA because they possessed special skills in what is categorized as high stakes interrogation. Jessen was on the bigger side than Mitchell, and he carried a cropped military haircut. He also did not speak in public- terse and guarded might describe him properly.

Following the fall of the towers, tehir first assignment was to assist in the interrogation of Abu Zubadayah. Zubadayah was one of the first high-level Al-Qaeda operatives to be captured. And over the years, they would go on interrogating other top Al-Qaeda suspected terrorists. of all these suspects, KSM was the biggest fish.

Mitchell recalled that KSM struck him as a brilliant fellow. He said he would ask KSM a question, and KSM would respond saying if he were in Mitchell's sit, that was not the question he would ask. He would then go on to offer Mitchell a question, which Mitchell would throw back at KSM. This question often had more detailed and global answers, compared to the initial question that Mitchell had in mind to ask him. One thing Mitchell particularly said was that if not for his capture,

KSM had all sorts of plans after the 9/11 attack. He described without reservation the attacks that were in the pipeline, adding that he thinks about economy of scale even when it comes to killing people.

Mitchell got creeped out the most when KSM spoke about Daniel Pearl. Mitchell cried, and he still does. Pearl was the Wall Street Journal reporter who was kidnapped in Pakistan in 2002, and later killed. Without being asked, KSM brought the subject up, stood up from his chair, and without emotions, he relived the technique he had used in killing Pearl. What Mitchell found particularly horrific about the entire episode was that KSM kept referring to Pearl as Daniel, as though he had some intimate relationship with the late reporter.

However, all of these were later, when KSM had opened up. When Mitchell and Jessen first confronted him in March 2003, things were very different. At that time, Mitchell said they had credible evidence that Al Qaeda was coming up with another big wave of attacks. They knew that Osama Bin Laden had met with Pakistani scientists who ere passing out nuclear technology. They also knew that the scientists had told Bin Laden that the biggest problem was getting the nuclear material, to which Bin Laden gave a response that suggested that he had already gotten it. This singular event sent the entire intelligence community into a frenzy.

Because of this, the CIA had people everywhere, looking for a dirty bomb. Washington was on high alert. Hence, when KSM was first captured, they felt that if anyone ought to now anything about the planned attacks, it had to be him. Unfortunately, however, KSM refused to talk, and Mitchell was not optimistic.

The very first set of interrogators that were hired to question KSM tried to do it the friendly way, by making him comfortable and brewing him tea. They even asked him respectful questions. But they got nowhere with that. KSM simply looked at them and continued to rock, back and forth.

Afterwards, KSM was handed over to someone Mitchell described as the news sheriff in town. He was an interrogator who had become a sadist. He contorted KSM into various types of stress positions. According to the interrogator, he had learned his approaches in South America from the communist rebels. Mitchell then added that the interrogator had gotten into a war of wills with KSM, holding that KSM wanted to be called sir, and that was all that he focused on. After trying for a week, he gave up, and KSM was handed over to Mitchell and Jessen.

The happenings afterwards are controversial. The methods of interrogation used on KSM have been a subject of debate for quite some time. Those that approve of those measures refer to them as enhanced interrogation techniques. Those that do not refer to them as torture. For now, let us dwell on what KSM's interrogation can tell us about both puzzles.

The deception of Ana Montes and Bernie Madoff, the confusion that was in paly over Amanda Knox's case, Graham Spanier's plight and Emily Doe are all pointer to the foundational problem that we have in making sense of persons that we do not know. Defaulting to truth is a critically important strategy that sometimes, and inescapably leads us astray. Transparency on the other hand is a commonsense assumption which has turned out to be more of an illusion. Both concepts however pose the same question: having accepted our shortcomings, what then should we do? There is the most extreme version of talking to strangers, and it is about a terrorist who wants to hold on to his secrets, and an interrogator who is willing to go to any length to let those secrets out.

CHAPTER 10: SYLVIA PLATH

KEY TAKEAWAYS

- Sylvia Plath lived in W.B. Yeats' house.
- Plath was on her way to becoming one of the world's most celebrated poets in the world.
- Plath took her own life.

Sometime in the fall of 1962, Sylvia Plath left her cottage for London. She felt she needed a fresh start in life. Her husband had abandoned her, and left her for another woman. She was all alone with their two small children. Somewhere in London's Primrose Hill neighborhood, she found an apartment. She wrote to her mother, telling her how excited she was to be writing from London, and that she was living in W.B. Yeats' house.

Early in the morning while her kids slept, she would write. Her productivity was superb. By December, she had finished a poetry collection, which her publisher told her should win the Pulitzer prize. Steadily, Plath was on her way to becoming one of the world's most celebrated young poets in the world.

In late December, a very deadly cold came down on England. In three hundred years, this was one of the most terrible winters. Soon, snow began to fall non-stop. People skated on the Thames. Everything froze, water pipes inclusive. There were lots of power outages, and leakages as well. Labor strikes also came up. All her life, Plath had struggled with depression and this time, it returned. Her friend and literary critic, Alfred Alvarez came visiting her on Christmas eve. He reported in his memoir, The Savage God, that she seemed different. According to him, she usually wore her hair in a bun, but this time around, it was loose. With her hair falling straight to her waist, she looked pale and empty. He added that when she walked in front of him, her hair gave off a very strong and sharp smell.

Her apartment was cold, and quite spare. Alvarez described it as being barely furnished and with very little in the way of Christmas decorations or her kids. Alvarez went on to write that Christmas is usually a bad time for the unhappy. He added that the false jollity that hits unhappy people from every corner makes depression and loneliness very hard to bear. Alvarez said he had never seen Plath so strained.

They each had a glass of wine, and as usual, she read her latest poems to him. He described those poems as being dark. With the new year, the weather became worse. Plath quarreled with her ex-husband, and fired her au pair. At some point, she carried her kids and went to live with Jillian and Garry Becker. They lived nearby. She told them she felt terrible. That day was a Thursday. And on Friday, she wrote to her ex-husband, Ted Hughes. Ted would later call this note a farewell note. On Sunday, she insisted that Gerry Becker drive her and her kids back to their apartment. Becker left her early in the evening after she had put the kids to bed. In the course of the next few hours, she left some food and water for her children in their room, and opened the window in her bedroom. She also wrote her doctor's name out along with a telephone number, and taped it to the baby carriage in the hallway. Then, she took with her towels, dishcloth and tape and she sealed the kitchen door. Next thing she did was to turn the gas in her kitchen stove on, and she placed her head inside the oven and killed herself.

It is no cliché to say that poets die young. As a matter of fact, the average life expectancy of poets is quite lower than those of actors, playwrights, novelists and nonfiction writers. Poets have higher rates of emotional disorders than actors, musicians and composers do. Of all occupations, poets have the highest suicide rates, fives times more than the general population. There is something about poetry that seems to either attract wounded people, or open up new wounds.

Plath was deeply obsessed about suicide; so much that she even wrote about it. She thought about it in the same tone with which she talked about any other risky event. According to Alvarez, Plath viewed death as a physical challenge which she had to overcome, and fulfilled every criterion of elevated suicide risk. She had even tried it before. She had once been a mental patient. She had lived in a culture foreign to her, even as an American, and this had dislocated her from her friends and family members. By a man she loved and idolized, she had been abandoned.

The night she died, Plath had left her coat and keys behind at the Beckers'. Jillian Becker, who wrote a book on Plath, as has everyone who knew Plath, said that was a sign of Plath's decision being final. Of course, she did not expect that Jillian nor Gerry would come after her during the night with her coat and keys. She did not want to be saved at the last moment from a death she wanted to inflict on herself.

When people look at Sylvia Plath's poetry and her history, they think they understand her, but in actual sense, there is something everyone is forgetting, and it is the third mistake we make with strangers.

In the years that followed the First World War, lots of British homes began using town gas to power their stoves and water heaters, the town gas was manufactured from col and a mixture of a variety of several compounds, which included the very deadly and odor free carbon monoxide. The fact that carbon monoxide was one of the compounds present gave everyone a simple means of killing themselves right inside their homes. In many cases, victims were found with their heads covered with coats or blankets, and with the tube from a gas tap brought under the edge of the covering article.

The year before Plath took her life- 1962 had five thousand, five hundred and eighty- eight people in England and Wales committed suicide. And out of those thousand, five hundred and eighty- eight people, two thousand, four hundred and sixty-nine of them did so just like Sylvia Plath did. Carbon-monoxide poisoning was by then the leading cause of lethal self-harm in the United Kingdom. Nothing else; not overdosing on pills or jumping off a bridge came close.

Within the same period however, the British gas industry took a turn. Town gas became very expensive and dirty. A discovery of large reserves of natural gas was made in the North Sea, and it was only a matter of time before a decision was reached to convert the country from Town gas to natural gas. To do this, every appliance in England either had to be replaced, or at least, upgraded. At the time, an official called it the greatest peacetime operation in this nation's history.

CHAPTER 11: CASE STUDY THE KANSAS CITY EXPERIMENTS

KEY TAKEAWAYS

- Preventive patrol for crime reduction.
- No one had ever written anything about police tactics.
- Those in areas where patrol was beefed up did not feel any safer than those in areas without patrol

About a century ago, a key figure in the American law enforcement known as O.W Wilson came up with the idea of what was known as preventive patrol. He believed that having police cars in unpredictable yet constant motion throughout the city would stop, or reduce crime. He felt that any criminal would always wonder whether or not a police car was just around the corner.

Now think about it. When you walk down your street, do you feel like the police are just around the next turn? Cities are large, and it does not feel that even a force as large as a police force could ever create the impression that they were everywhere.

This was the dilemma that faced the Kansas City Police Department in the early 1970s. the department was about to hire extra police officers, but there were several questions as to how to deploy them. They were torn in between following Wilson's advice or having the police officers assigned to specific locations, like schools and difficult neighborhoods. In order to resolve the question, they hired a criminologist named George Kelling.

Kelling said that a certain group mentioned that riding around in cars does not improve anything, while another group said it was absolutely essential. And because of this, he had to be brought in.

Kelling had an idea which was to select fifteen beats from the southern part of the city and divide them into three different groups. Of the three groups, one would be the control group. As usual, police work would continue as it always had in that neighborhood. In the second neighborhood, Kelling would have no preventive patrol, but instead police officers would only respond when they were called. And in the third, he would double, and sometime, triple the number of squad cars on the street.

Kelling noted that nothing like this had ever been done in the history of policing. No one had ever written anything about police tactics. O.W Wilson and people like him had hunches here and there. But in its entirety, the police job was considered an art, and not a science that could be assessed. Kelling mentioned that many people told him his experiment would fail, and that the police weren't ready for research. He was told he wouldn't be able to do it, and that the police would sabotage it. But Kelling already had the backing of Kansas City Police chief. The chief had built his career in the FBI, and he was shocked when he found out that police departments knew very little about what they did. He admitted much later that many of them in the department often felt they were training, equipping and deploying men to do a job that neither them nor anyone else knew much about.

Kelling ran the experiment for a whole year, and diligently collected every statistic he could get on crime within the three areas of study. The result showed nothing. Burglaries remained the same in all three neighborhoods, as much as robberies, auto-thefts and vandalism. Those in areas where patrol was beefed up did not feel any safer than those in areas without patrol. As a matter of fact, they almost did not notice what had happened. All the results were in just one direction, which was basically the fact that it all made no difference. Nothing mattered; not to citizens, not even to crime statistics.

Everyone in Kansas read the results. At the initial stage. there was some disbelief. Some of the police departments in the urban areas remained committed to Wilson's idea. As a matter of fact, the Los Angeles Police Chief stood up at a conference and said that if the findings were true, then every officer in Kansas was asleep, assuring them that the case was not the same in Los Angeles.

Slowly however, resistance paved the way to resignation. The study came out as violent crime was beginning its long, hard, two-decade surge across the United States, and it fed into the growing feeling among people in law enforcement that the task before them was overwhelming. They had thought they could prevent crime with police patrols, but with the Kansas City Police Department testing that assumption empirically, they had discovered it was nothing more than a charade.

CHAPTER 12: SANDRA BLAND

KEY TAKEAWAYS

- Bland was stopped because she failed to signal the lane change.
- Encinia's first mistake was failing to let things die down.
- Encinia's second mistake was talking in an assertive tone.
- Encinia's third mistake was snapping.

On July 10, 2015, at 4:27, Sandra Bland got pulled over by a Texas State Trooper in Texas. She was driving a silver Azera with Illinois license plates. At the time, she was twenty-eight years old and had just come from Chicago to start a job at Prairie View University, the officer was named Brian Encinia. He parked behind her and approached her, and spoke then spoke to her through the open passenger window.

Encinia explained to her that he had stopped her because she failed to signal the lane change. He then proceeded to ask if she had her driver's license and registration with her. He also asked how long she had been in Texas. Bland responded that she only got in the day before. He requested for her driver's license whilst asking where she was headed to. She handed him her license which he took to his patrol car. A few minutes later, he returned and Bland explained that she was waiting on him to let her go. Encinia asks if something was wrong with her because she sounded irritated. Bland responded saying she was actually very irritated, and that she had no idea what she was getting a ticket for. She argued that Encinia was speeding up and tailing her, and that she decided to change lanes, and then, he stopped her. She then added that the fact that she was irritated was not going to stop him from giving her a ticket anyway.

Now this is Encinia's first mistake. He could have tried to let things die down. In the course of the investigation, it was discovered that Encinia actually never meant to give her a ticket, but a warning. He could have simply told her that. But he did not. He could have explained carefully to her that she ought to have signaled, and provided her with reasons as well. He could have even gone on to smile or joke with her, and acknowledge that he was listening to her. But he does none of these, and instead, he waits for an uncomfortable moment to strike. He goes on to ask her if she was done, and she said she was. She actually was. She had told him how irritated she was, and next thing Bland does is to take out a cigarette and light it, trying to calm her nerves. In the video, none of these were even seen. All that was seen was the back of her car and Encinia, standing by her door. If you stopped the tape there and showed it to 100 people, 99 would guess that's where it ends. But it doesn't.

Encinia asked Bland if she would mind putting out her cigarette, in a flat, assertive tone. This was his second mistake. He should have paused and allowed Bland get herself together. Bland retorted that she was in her car, and asked him why she had to put out her cigarette. And she was right. A police officer did not have the right to tell anyone not to smoke. He should simply have told her she was right, and ask if she would mind waiting till they were done. He could have even dropped the issue altogether. But he does not. There was something about the tone of her voice that gets Encinia back up, and he feels that his authority has been severely challenged. Then he snaps- his third mistake made.

From then onward, Encinia forced Bland out of her car, and knocked her head into the ground. Bland, says she has epilepsy. Encinia offers no response and places her under arrest- for doing next to nothing. Bland was taken into custody on the grounds of felony assault charges. Three days after her arrest, she was found dead in her cell, hanging from a noose fashioned from a plastic bag. After a short investigation, Encinia was fired on the grounds that he had violated Chapter 5, Section 05.17.00, of the Texas State Trooper General Manual which states that any employee of the Department of Public safety shall be courteous to the public and other employees; dutifully perform his assigned duties, control behavior, exercise patience and discretion, and shall not engage in argumentative discussions, regardless of the provocation, howbeit extreme.

Brian Encinia was a bully. The lesson of what happened on the afternoon of July 10, 2015, is that when police talk to strangers, they need to be respectful and polite.

But this is wrong.

Made in the USA
Coppell, TX
27 February 2020

16246162R00037